Beware of Bears!

By Vivian French

Illustrated by Cate James

W

FRANKLIN WATTS

LONDON • SYDNEY

The Stone Age Family

Little Nut

Pim

Tall Cousin

Pod

Old Boulder

Chapter One

"NOT FAIR!" Little Nut yelled. "Want to

go FISHING!"

"Me too," said Pim. "Why can't we come?"

Tall Cousin frowned. "Only big boys go night fishing. No girls, no little ones. Just me and Pod." He picked Little Nut up and dropped him down next to Old Boulder who was dozing by the fire. "Stay here!"

Old Boulder opened one eye. "Watch out for bears. They like night fishing too."

Pod clutched at his spear. "Bears?"

"If you don't bother them, they won't bother you," Tall Cousin told him. "I thought everyone knew that."

Old Boulder grunted and closed his eyes.

Tall Cousin looked at Pod. "I've been night fishing LOADS of times," he boasted. "I catch lots of fish!"

"I will too," said Pod. Tall Cousin folded his arms. "But I'll catch the most! I'm the oldest!"

"Big deeds are better than big words," said Old Boulder, but only Pim heard him. Tall Cousin wasn't listening. He and Pod were marching away, and Tall Cousin was whistling loudly.

Pim watched them go. "They're making a lot of noise," she said.

Little Nut didn't answer and "HARRUMPH ..." Old Boulder was snoring.

Pim looked round to see what Little Nut was doing – and he wasn't there.

"Oh no!" Pim squinted into the moonlight. A small determined figure was stamping after Pod and Tall Cousin.

"Little Nut!" Pim shouted, and she went running after her brother.

Chapter Two

Tall Cousin led the way down the hill, Pod
hurrying behind him.

"Old Boulder worries too much," Tall Cousin
said. "I've NEVER seen a bear when I've
been night fishing."

"What would we do if we did?" Pod asked.

Tall Cousin laughed. "Oh, we'd just climb a tree and wait for it to go away." Pod looked anxiously over his shoulder. "Perhaps we shouldn't talk so loudly."

"I told you," Tall Cousin said. "There aren't any bears here."

He shrugged. "I wouldn't have asked you to come if I'd known you were a scaredy cat." Pod didn't answer and they went on walking in silence. Behind them, Little Nut nodded wisely. "Climb trees," he said to himself.

Once they had reached the bottom of the hill, Tall Cousin led the way into a dark wood. There were strange noises all around and Pod held his breath. RUSTLE RUSTLE! Pod pulled at Tall Cousin's arm. "I think something's following us…"

"It's only the wind," Tall Cousin told him.

"It might be a bear!" Pod was peering into the darkness.

"Stop fussing, Pod! Bears make LOADS of noise." Tall Cousin pointed ahead.

"Look! That's where we're going fishing!" Tall Cousin was right. The sea was shining brightly in the moonlight beyond the trees.

"WOW!" breathed Pod. "WOW!"

"Come on!" Tall Cousin waved his spear in the air. "I'll race you! Last one there's a loser!" He dashed away, and Pod chased after him.

Chapter Three

Pim saw them go and waited to see if Little
Nut appeared. She had lost sight of him in
the wood and now she was worried. What
had happened to him? Where could he be?

OUCH! Something had fallen on her head. Pim looked up and saw Little Nut grinning down at her. Beside him was a pile of fir cones. "Climb tree!" he ordered. Pim was about to argue when she heard a snuffling noise. It wasn't far away and her heart suddenly began to beat much faster.

With a spring and a scramble, she climbed her way through the branches to reach Little Nut.

"Bear," he said cheerfully. "Big bear."

Pim stared into the darkness. Little Nut was right. A huge bear was wandering along between the trees sniffing and snuffling and peering this way and that.

"Throw cones?" Little Nut asked hopefully.
Pim shook her head and, as quietly as she
could, climbed further up the tree. The
moon was very bright, and as she got
higher she could easily see the seashore.
Tall Cousin was wading into the waves
and Pod was close behind him.

SPLASH! Tall Cousin had hurled his spear into the water. A moment later he was pulling out a huge silver fish. He threw it onto the beach. "See?" he said. "Easy peasy!"

Pod took a deep breath. "Here goes!" he said and stabbed with his spear – SPLASH! He'd caught a fish! Not a very big one, but a real fish. "YES!" he shouted.

Tall Cousin laughed. "That's just a tiddler! Look! Do it like this!" He whirled his spear round his head, and – SPLASH! Another big fish. He turned to throw it onto the beach "OOOOOOH!"

Tall Cousin and Pod stared in horror. Pim, up in her tree, stared too. The huge black bear was walking down from the wood. It saw the fish on the beach and grunted happily. A moment later, it was helping itself to a free dinner. Pod's eyes were wide. "What are we going to do?" he whispered.

Tall Cousin didn't say anything. His teeth were chattering and he was very pale.

Chapter Four

Pim put her fingers in her mouth and whistled as loudly as she could. The bear looked up, puzzled, and stared at the wood.

Pod grabbed Tall Cousin's arm. "Quick!" he whispered. "The bear's looking the other way! Head for the side of the beach! We can creep up beside the rocks!"

"I can't!" wailed Tall Cousin. "I'm scared!"

"Yes, you can!" shouted Pod. He half pushed, half pulled Tall Cousin through the water towards the rocks that edged the shore.

Pim kept whistling, but the bear grew bored.
It dropped its head and began to eat again.
Pim could see the boys, and she guessed
what they were planning, but how could she
keep the bear facing the other way?

"Cones," said a small voice, and Little Nut was beside her.

"CLEVER Little Nut," Pim said. There were plenty all around her and she gathered a handful. Taking careful aim, she sent a fir cone whizzing through the air. It fell beside the bear, and the animal bent down to see what it was.

GRRR

"Now!" breathed Pod, and he began to tiptoe up the sand, dragging Tall Cousin with him. Up, and up they crept, until they were almost level with the bear. Tiptoe, tiptoe –

"Oooops!" gasped Tall Cousin, and he sneezed. "Achooooo!"

"Grrrrrr?" The bear swung round.

PLOP! A shower of fir cones came flying down and the bear turned back, rubbing its ears. More cones followed, and the bear shook its head. Then, with a grunt, it picked up the last fish and went shambling away in the opposite direction.

Heaving a huge sigh of relief, Pod and Tall Cousin reached the edge of the wood. Tall Cousin didn't stop there, though. While shouting, "Help! Bears!" he ran away as fast as he could, crashing through the bushes without looking back.

Chapter Five

Pim, Pod and Little Nut hugged each other very, VERY hard.

"And now we'd better go home," Pim said.

"Old Boulder might think we've been eaten by a bear."

"Oh!" Little Nut suddenly looked very guilty,

but Pim put her arm round him.

"It's all right. You're a hero, Little Nut!"

"So are you," Pod told her.

Pim giggled. "We're ALL heroes!"

"Tall Cousin isn't," Pod said, and they were

all smiling as they made their way safely

home ... and found Old Boulder still asleep.

Stone Age Facts

The Stone Age began around 2.6 million years ago. It is called the Stone Age as people used tools and weapons made of stone. Using sharp spears and fishing hooks, they hunted fish and animals but had to watch out for the wild, wandering bears! Stone Age families would also feast on wild boar, nuts and berries, or whatever food they could find.

Franklin Watts
First published in Great Britain in 2015 by
The Watts Publishing Group

Text © Vivian French 2015
Illustrations © Cate James 2015

Series Editor: Melanie Palmer
Series Advisor: Catherine Glavina
Series Designers: Peter Scoulding
and Cathryn Gilbert

ISBN 978 1 4451 4270 8 (hbk)
ISBN 978 1 4451 4272 2 (pbk)
ISBN 978 1 4451 4271 5 (library ebook)

Printed in China

MIX
Paper from
responsible sources
FSC
www.fsc.org
FSC® C104740

Franklin Watts
An imprint of
Hachette Children's Group
Part of The Watts Publishing Group
Carmelite House
50 Victoria Embankment
London EC4Y 0DZ

An Hachette UK Company
www.hachette.co.uk

www.franklinwatts.co.uk